TEST YOUR EMOTIONS

by

CHRISTOPHER MARKERT

A. THOMAS AND COMPANY
Wellingborough, Northamptonshire

First published in the United Kingdom 1980

ISBN 0 85454 073 3

Photoset by
Specialised Offset Services Ltd., Liverpool
and printed in Great Britain by
Hunt Barnard Printing Ltd., Aylesbury, Bucks.

1. How to Test Your Emotions

How do you really feel, right now? A simple question, but one that few people can answer accurately. We may say that we are annoyed with a neighbour, tired of work, happy in a new home and so on. However, our feelings are not primarily governed by our environment — people, work, homes, etc. — but by our reactions to these things. And our reactions are influenced by deep-seated, often unsuspected emotions. To know how we truly feel at any given moment, we must know what these emotions are.

For instance, there are many logical ways to handle an annoying neighbour. We can tell her what is bothering us; we can avoid her; or we can decide that the problem is not worth our attention at all. But if we suffer in silence, inwardly fuming, our problem is not our neighbour, but the emotions that make us react to her as we do.

THE SYMBOLS

The abstract symbols on the next page can help you define the hidden feelings that mould your life at any given time. You will find that your attitude towards them changes surprisingly often, within weeks or days, and sometimes even within hours. This means that you will look up a different test result almost every time you consult the book.

The eight symbols have an uncanny ability to make you aware of answers that are already dormant within you. They can bring out suppressed emotions and lead them into constructive channels. Quite often they can actually turn a problem into an asset or a pleasant challenge. They can help you to overcome hang-ups and make better use of your potential. These symbols are a better test of your emotions than any set of identifiable objects or shapes. Because they are abstract, you will react to them spontaneously, with a minimum of outside associations, even if you see them very often.

Consult the symbols whenever you are confronted with a decision or a problem, when you need a fresh perspective, or when you simply feel out of tune with your world. The interpretations can be your constant counsellors in the years to come. Almost every time you open the book, your attitude towards the symbols has changed somewhat and so has your test result. (You will find this hard to believe at first). Consequently you will never get the feeling of having been permanently labelled.

The book can serve as an 'instant problem solver' in all areas of your life, at home, at work and in your relationships with others. Even money problems become more manageable after the symbols have been consulted. This is because money in itself is rarely a problem — but your present attitude towards money may be.

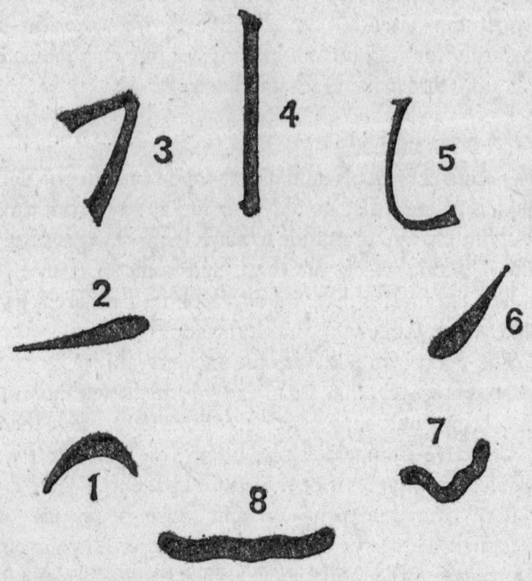

The book can do different things for different people, depending on their needs, desires and circumstances. A housewife may find that it helps her to create a better atmosphere in the home. An executive may use the book to gain promotion or to find a more satisfying career. A scientist may discover that the interpretations help him solve complex abstract problems. A girl may find that the book helps her to have a better relationship with her boy friend. Others will discover that their lives become more rewarding and enjoyable after they have used the symbol test over a period of time.

Of these eight symbols, make a spontaneous choice of the one you like most and the one you like least. To find out what your choice reveals about your present state of mind, simply combine the numbers of the selected symbols, most-liked first, least-liked second. For example, if you liked symbol 2 and disliked symbol 7, turn to interpretation number 27.

YOUR CHANGING EMOTIONS

Feelings are rarely static. Circumstances change; goals shift, and our feelings shift with them. The qualities that you want today may not be the same ones that you will need tomorrow, next month or next year. Solve one set of problems and — such is life — sooner or later a new crop will appear. We cannot protect ourselves from all difficulties for all time; but we can learn to handle them in the most efficient way possible. The 56 interpretations in this book can help you to understand your fluctuating emotions as they occur — and their relation to each new set of circumstances.

. You should have changing likes and dislikes among the symbols; this indicates living flexibility and growth. If you find yourself liking one symbol consistently and ignoring the others, this is a warning signal that you are becoming rigid, that your life is stagnant and one-dimensional. Let yourself grow!*

* Another book by the same author explains all this in detail: *Let Yourself Grow* (Wildwood House Ltd., London, 1978).

Each new choice leads to a new analysis of your current emotional state. The secret fears, hidden conflicts and rigid thought patterns that have troubled you become clear. Each interpretation helps you to look at yourself, and your situation, from a different angle; new ideas begin to flow and new solutions present themselves.

This is therefore not a personality test that reveals your permanent character traits, although many people cannot believe this at first. To solve most problems you do not have to change your character (or the world). You only need to correct the bias in your present attitude — and the book shows you how.

This applies even to past problems. It is only too human to blame the past (about which you can do nothing) for a present problem about which you *can* do something. Your brain is perfectly capable of fabricating a biased and partly fictitious picture of the past (or future) that supports your present attitude of self-pity and complacency. (Even Freud admitted this in his later works.) The focal point of your life is not your past or your future, but your present, and it is what you do now that counts. We only live in the present and 'the future never comes'. Your life is right as long as your current attitude towards present, past and future is right. This statement only seems incredible because you are not normally aware of your attitude or the fault in it. This is why the symbol test is so important — it increases your awareness.

YOUR RELATIONSHIPS, YOUR BODY AND YOUR HAPPINESS

This test can help resolve conflicts between people, as well as inner conflicts. When differences arise at home, at work or anywhere else, everyone involved would benefit from taking the test. Some will prefer to look up their test result privately, so that others will not see their weakness — and this is perfectly natural. In any case, they will then get a better idea of how their own unrealistic attitude contributes to the misunderstanding. Often this will uncover the root of the problem instantly and clear the way for its resolution.

Incidentally, you may like to have your family and friends choose their most-liked and least-liked symbols even if there is no conflict between you. The interpretation of their choices will help them understand themselves better, and help you to understand them too.

You will find that part of each interpretation refers to your body's co-ordination. You may not realize it, but your movements – how you walk, sit, stand, the gestures you make – reflect your state of mind. For example, when you feel tense and nervous your movements will also be tense and nervous in some way. You will not be able to relax mentally until you relax physically. But if you change your movements so that they reflect the quality you want to achieve (as represented by the most liked symbol), you will feel better immediately. Changing your physical attitude can be the first step towards changing your mental attitude.

Now take another look at the eight symbols. Decide, within about one minute, how many of them you dislike or find objectionable. The more figures you dislike, the more doubts, inner conflicts and problems you are experiencing. On the other hand, you can observe that conflicts and problems tend to disappear or get solved as you begin to accept an increasing number of figures. The more figures you like or accept, the better you feel, the better the world looks. to you and the happier and 'luckier' you will tend to be at the moment.

Whenever you feel really happy, you find all of the figures more or less agreeable, although you still have preferences. During such periods, everything within you and outside you seems to fall into place spontaneously. Problem solving becomes a pleasure and the world makes sense. You are functioning well and using your full potential. Most likely you are in love with somebody, or in any case you are 'in love with life'.

Needless to say, this subtle balance is seldom attained and easily lost. But the symbols will help you to attain it more often! While you are in this state of mind, you no longer experience the polarity between the various symbols as negative or bothersome. You feel that each figure has some merit, and that together they form an integrated whole. Under such circumstances you have no need for this book — until the next problem crops up and you begin to dislike some of the figures again.

HOW THE TEST WORKS

Each of the eight symbols suggests a certain quality. When you prefer that symbol, you indicate that you feel this quality is missing from your life *now*, and that you would like to develop it. When you dislike a symbol, you feel that you have too much of the quality it suggests. These are very personal choices. You want the preferred quality for your own peace of mind, not because it benefits your friends, family or the world. You reject the disliked quality because it disturbs *you*, not because it disturbs others.

What does each symbol mean? This depends on whether you like it or not, and on which other symbol you dislike (or like). Thus each symbol has 14 different meanings (2 x 7), and you find them described in the interpretations.

It is essential that we have goals and preferences, of course. Without them, we would fritter our life away in aimless wandering. However, problems arise when we pursue one quality (as indicated by the most-liked symbol) to the extent that we begin to suppress another (the least-liked symbol). When this happens, we must face the quality we have ignored and learn to re-incorporate it into our lives in a way that restores our mental balance.

Your choice of symbols, then, reveals the desires, aversions, fears and hopes that make you feel as you do at the very moment you take the test. Certain potential conflicts and obstacles also become evident from your combination of symbols. Thus, this test can help you discover not only what you want, but what prevents you from having it. When you turn to your interpretation, you will find practical, tailor-made information on where you stand — right now — and what you can do about it!

2. Interpretations

You would rather indulge in poetic fantasies than face facts right now. You want to enjoy the moment, not strive for future happiness. However, only those who really feel rather grim — as you do — will join you in your daydreams. Others sense that you are neglecting opportunities and that secretly you are worried about the future.

Although the world seems very solemn and businesslike to you now, the factors that stop you from leading a more idyllic life are also in yourself. You cannot slow down — or get out of the 'rat race' — so you dislike haste and ambition in others. It will probably take a few weeks to change these old habits, but the day will come when you no longer seek fantasies because you have added the necessary poetic touches to your real life. Your worried state of mind shows in your restless body movements. Try to move less nervously.

Your search for fantasy could make you aimless or unrealistic. Remember to take time out to do necessary work and to try to get ahead; put a foundation under your dream castle. If you find yourself in surroundings where materialistic goals prevail, do not try to escape into a make-believe world of your own. Instead, approach your daily life with vision and imagination; try to perform your duties with more inventiveness. In this way, you will be neither an idle dreamer nor a superficial opportunist.

Your objective: **Concentrate on those dreams that can be turned into reality easily. Keep moving towards a promising future while enjoying the present. You can be idealistic and realistic at the same time. In your dealings with others, work out a joint approach that is imaginative but also goal-orientated.**

Your present desire is to be good-natured and generous, to enjoy friendship rather than power. You think it is better to be deceived than to deceive. Your loved ones probably encourage your attempts at kindness, but they will also warn you not to become ineffectual. They sense your tendency toward exaggerated generosity — and your hidden toughness.

You consider yourself a benevolent person, but some of your old habits are really quite demanding. Secretly, you do not want to give away anything that you might need for yourself; you dislike toughness partly because you cannot be generous without an ulterior motive. To some extent, your present concern with kindness is caused by your unsuccessful attempts to control these selfish traits. But keep trying, and in a few weeks the day will come when you can practise true kindness.

Your tense body movements also indicate that you are still too hard and grim under the surface. Try letting yourself move more softly and spontaneously.

If you find that your emphasis on generosity makes you weak or helpless, bring some determination back into your life. Take what you deserve; forge ahead firmly. Then you can show kindness when it is appropriate. Do not let others take advantage of you; if you do, you will lose your self-respect and self-reliance. However, be careful that you do not swing to the other extreme and become ruthless.

Your objective: **Be kind but not ineffectual. Learn to be generous without forgetting your legitimate rights. When working with others, approach problems with determination but in a pleasant manner.**

At the moment you want to see joy rather than duty in life; you feel that people would be happier if they were more flexible, friendly and informal. Your attempts to be warm and affectionate are probably appreciated by your loved ones, but they may sense your lack of discipline — coupled with a hidden stiffness.

The rigidity and coldness that bother you are not only in your environment, but also in yourself. Some of your habits are still rather stuffy and tense. You dislike sober principles and naked facts partly because of your unsuccessful attempts to loosen up your own inner stiffness. However, if you keep trying, eventually you will no longer have to *act* naturally because you will be natural.

Try to let your body move more spontaneously too; right now your movements are very wooden.

Until a more relaxed attitude becomes habitual, you may overshoot the mark at times and become emotional and childish. If this happens, revive your sense of responsibility. Make yourself face reality and do neglected chores. Everybody needs play, imagination and satisfaction, but your present dissatisfaction with a sober life and strict duties could lead you into rejecting all responsibility. Instead, work at a task you enjoy, face its unpleasant phases and · try to accomplish worthwhile goals. This will bring you more joy than idleness ever will.

Your objective: **Enjoy life in a responsible way. Do your duty, but with imagination and cheerfulness. Others will drop their stuffy pose if you find a joint approach that is both natural and responsible.**

<table><tr><td>15</td><td>ENTHUSIASM</td><td>⌒</td><td>Ɩ</td></tr></table>

You would like to enjoy life without reservations and deal with others without suspicion or calculation. Analysis kills enthusiasm, you feel, and you want to have enough faith to rise above prevailing doubts. Your friends will probably encourage your attempts at exuberance, but they will also admonish you not to become too gullible. They know that you can get carried away by your fervour, and that secretly you are uncertain about many things.

You would like to see more enthusiasm around you, but how about having some yourself? Some of your old habits and attitudes are quite hesitant. Your present interest in enthusiasm stems, in part, from your inability to show unreserved feelings. You fear criticism partly because it reinforces your hidden doubts. It will take a few weeks to overcome these uncertainties and restraints, but with practice, you will soon learn to express your true feelings.

Your body reflects your mind's reluctant attitude; try to be more lively in your movements.

Until enthusiasm becomes a habit, you may sometimes overreach yourself and become too emotional or unquestioning. To counteract this, occasionally make yourself think, doubt and investigate. Base your actions on experience rather than impulse. By periodic self-criticism and unprejudiced fact-probing, you will avoid the extremes of either believing everything or believing nothing.

Your objective: **Be enthusiastic without becoming naïve. By welcoming justified doubts you can enjoy life in a sensible way. Enjoy the roses but keep in mind that every rose has its thorn. In your dealings with others, try to arrive at a common approach that is cheerful but does not disregard their experience or dignity.**

At present you want to be bright and cheerful, to keep hoping when things look gloomy. You probably think that brooding over past mistakes or searching for profound wisdom will only depress you. Those close to you may encourage your attempts to be cheerful, but they are worried that you may become slightly clownish or flippant.

Actually, you have an inner melancholy — an inability to enjoy life — that is partly the reason for your present preoccupation with enjoyment. As long as you must search for pleasure, you are an apprentice at the art of happiness. But if you keep trying, you should be able to overcome your hidden sadness in a few weeks.

You need to change your heavy, dragging body movements, too. Try to let your limbs move more lightly and you will start to feel less weighed down.

In your efforts to dispel your inner gloom, you may go to another extreme and become frivolous or too hopeful. That is the time to come down from the clouds and ponder the true meaning of things. Try to add some depth to your happiness and some basis to your hopes. Both wisdom and cheerfulness are important in life; each depends on, and is enhanced by, the other. Cheerfulness achieved at the expense of wisdom is artificial and will collapse, but happiness based on inner strength and understanding will endure.

Your objective: **Be cheerful without becoming superficial. Do not become careless in your optimism. See the deeper meaning in life without getting weighed down. Others will joyfully co-operate with you when they see that you are aware of the more serious aspects of your joint project.**

<table>
<tr><td>**17**</td><td>*SUBLIMITY*</td><td>⌒</td><td>⌣</td></tr>
</table>

You would like to rise above everyday confusion and appreciate the sublime and beautiful right now. You probably admire things or people more noble than yourself, and look down on anyone whom you consider sensual or materialistic. Your admiration of the good may have a religious quality.

Have you noticed that others have little desire to be 'lifted-up'? That is because they do not feel as dragged down and confused as you do. The influences that stop you from raising your life to a higher level are not only in your environment—some of your own attitudes are rather base. An inner conflict between your noble and not-so-noble instincts is causing much of your confusion. It will take a few weeks to resolve matters, but if you keep trying, you will be able to rise above both internal and external disorder.

Your heavy, befuddled body movements are still at odds with your mind. Let your limbs move more lightly.

Be careful that your interest in lofty ideals does not make you condescending. Now and then, make it a point to do unpretentious, worldly things. By getting your feet on the ground again, you can discover your natural self. Avoid imposing restrictions on others; people must choose their own goals. And remember that although a high-minded life may require a control of sensual desires, it does not require their total suppression.

Your objective: **Raise your life to a higher level without losing touch with the earth below. Instead of repressing worldly joys and sensuous pleasures you can refine them. When working with others, tackle common problems in an inspiring yet practical way.**

You are now trying to put more interest and inspiration into a monotonous existence. You think that life should be full of wonderful, romantic experiences and you would like to find them. To your surprise, few people will share your feelings; most have their own interests and are not as bored as you are. Your loved ones may encourage your new projects, but they will also advise you to keep your feet on the ground. They fear that you may overcompensate for your hidden boredom by floating off on a cloud of whims.

Your efforts to make your surroundings more interesting must be accompanied by a more lively attitude on your part. Some of your old habits are quite dreary, and your dislike of monotony is partly caused by your unsuccessful attempts to overcome your own dullness.

Your body movements are still sleepy and heavy too. Your mind cannot be inspired if your body moves about dully.

It will probably take a few weeks to rouse your mind out of its hibernation. However, one day you will realize that you are no longer preoccupied with finding new and exciting things to do because you have become interested in life again. In the meantime, rest and calm down occasionally; do not pretend to have an interest in everything. If you reserve your attention for life's more worthwhile things, you can regain your peace of mind.

Your objective: **Be lively and interested while keeping your feet on the ground. You can enjoy life without becoming childish. Others will be more enthusiastic about your mutual project(s) when you find a joint approach that is inspiring yet balanced.**

You would like to see things as they are and you would rather act than dream. You want to engage in practical thought, not lofty speculations. Those close to you will encourage you to be more realistic, but they also feel that you are too hasty and unimaginative now. They sense your tendency to get carried away with ambitious plans — and that secretly you are unsure of your goals.

You are annoyed if others are not brisk and to the point, but you, too, find it hard to think and act decisively. You disapprove of fantasies partly because you cannot stop yourself from daydreaming. It will take you a few weeks to develop a more efficient attitude. But, with effort, you will be able to come down from the clouds.

It would help if you changed your vague physical movements into more swift, definite gestures. Try to walk faster and more often too.

In your attempts to face reality you may become too concerned with speed and materialistic goals. If that happens, get away from superficial hustle and bustle for a while; take some time to plan with imagination and scope. Once the grand design is plotted out, routine duties are done more easily. You may feel that you have been too aimless in the past, but if you move ahead thoughtlessly now, you will be disappointed; progress only benefits those with the imagination to use its results.

Your objective: **Take care of necessary business, but with imagination and enthusiasm. By giving a higher purpose to your projects you will find it easier to carry them out with efficiency and joy. Others will gladly co-operate when they sense that your approach is both realistic and imaginative.**

Right now you would like to proceed with ease, using your wits to avoid obstacles. Your friends probably appreciate your attempts to be more polished, but they will warn you not to be too easy-going. They know that you tend to be evasive, and that you have a hidden urge to use force.

Although you often find your progress impeded by awkward circumstances and clumsy people, you have some rough spots yourself. You dislike blundering or rude behaviour partly because of your frustrated attempts to control your own urge to get tough. It will be a few weeks before you can completely abandon your heavy-handed habits. But once you do, you will no longer need to strive for smoothness so single-mindedly.

Your body movements, too, are still ungainly. Try to make them more graceful and swift.

While you are trying to round off your rough edges, you may sometimes become too permissive or devious. You can change this by bringing some forcefulness back into your life. Be blunt occasionally; stand up to a challenge; show determination in the face of obstacles. Even the most intelligently planned path is rarely free of all roadblocks. Force and determination are needed sometimes. If you become too polite and accommodating in order not to offend, you may lose face and weaken your position.

Your objective: **Proceed with ease and intelligence, but be ready to remove obstacles that cannot be circumvented. By thus asserting yourself and regaining self-respect you can set the stage for streamlined progress. In your dealings with others, work out an intelligent plan that avoids friction where possible but does not dodge the issues.**

<table><tr><td>24</td><td>*PROGRESS*</td><td>→ |</td></tr></table>

You have a desire to move forward now, to stir up your stagnant environment and implement new ideas. You are suspicious of long-standing arrangements or institutions and dissatisfied with the established routine of your life. Close friends will encourage your eagerness to get things rolling, but they recognize that your enthusiasm for new ideas could lead you into superficial judgments now.

Actually, your desire for progress is mainly due to a feeling that your own affairs are not moving ahead fast enough. What you may not know is that some of your own conservative attitudes are holding you back. You dislike the existing order partly because you cannot break out from your own inhibitions. It will take you some weeks to overcome these old habits, but when you do, you will be able to get your projects moving.

Your stiff, restrained body movements reflect your inhibited state of mind. Let your body and limbs move more freely and swiftly.

Until a more progressive attitude becomes second nature, you may sometimes be too pushy or make changes just for the sake of change. Try to distinguish between transitory and lasting benefits as you move ahead.

Before you overturn existing rules and institutions, ask yourself what the consequences will be; let your conscience tell you if you are heading in the right direction.

Your objective: **Move forward without forgetting your need for stability. Keep your goal in mind and make needed changes, but do not sacrifice your principles. Others will go along with you when you allow them to make progress without hurting their integrity.**

You want to be as busy as possible — get everything done, take advantage of every opportunity — and earn some money too. Others may encourage your efforts to be active, but they also feel that you are worried, tired and lack charm at the moment.

You realize that things are progressing too slowly, but some of your own habits are inconsistent with your efforts to stay busy. Although you have spurts of energy, you seem unwilling to move most of the time. Your interest in hectic activity is partly caused by your inability to change your idle way of life. It will take a few weeks to overcome this, but if you persevere, one day you will discover that you are no longer trying to keep busy because you have plenty to do.

One way to change your mental habits is to change your weary physical habits. Why not move more swiftly and positively?

Until a more active way of life becomes natural to you, you may overdo it at times and become too hasty or aggressive. You can correct this by occasionally taking time to sit down and evaluate the results of your efforts. Try to keep things in perspective. Although you would like to provide material comforts for your loved ones, the accumulation of wealth, in itself, does not mean success. True success comes when material well-being and dignity are harmonized.

Your objective: **Move ahead with your projects without becoming hasty. Do things in an efficient but dignified way. When dealing with others, find an approach that is progressive but allows them to remain dignified human beings.**

<table><tr><td>26</td><td>OPTIMISM</td><td>—</td><td>╱</td></tr></table>

You are trying to take difficulties in your stride and make the best of circumstances now. You hope that there are enough opportunities around for someone with the ambition to use them, but you do not want to spend time analyzing your position. Too much deep thinking, you feel, leads to melancholy.

In spite of your surface optimism, there is a hidden pessimism inside you; you know that things are not going well — that something is pulling you down. This 'something' is not only outside yourself, but inside too. You really feel that you are expecting too much from life and this keeps you from all-out effort on any project. It will take several weeks to change your defeatist attitude, but you will be able to overcome it if you keep trying.

The sluggishness of your body has probably bothered you lately; if you move more lightly, you will feel less weighed down.

While you are trying to be more hopeful, you may exaggerate the attitude and become impatient or hasty. Force yourself to do a thorough job sometimes; with thought and a little plodding, you can build a sound foundation for your projects.

Deep down you may feel that you are on thin ice now, and must count on luck to save you from drowning. Perhaps you are trying to ignore a danger or sweep a problem under the carpet. But if you face reality, you will be better able to deal with it.

Your objective: **Be optimistic without expecting too much and without fearing failure. Keep going but do not become superficial in your planning. Others will support you if your approach is future-orientated but thorough.**

You are trying to organize and streamline the confusion around you now. You want to get started early, get more things done, and plan for future success. Wasted time or disorganized surroundings make you feel very uncomfortable. The people you love will probably encourage your efforts to put things in order, but they sense your tendency to overdo your planning — and your hidden aimlessness.

Part of your need for efficiency is caused by your own inability to get things rolling and you cannot always resist the temptation to loaf around. Once in a while you do get organized, but then you swing to another extreme and proceed mechanically. If you can set up a practical, unforced plan to live by, the confusion around you will fall into place naturally. Try this for a few weeks, and you will soon see that you are no longer concerned with efficiency because things are organized.

A certain laziness in your movements has undoubtedly bothered you lately. If you move your body more swiftly, your problems will be half-solved.

You may tend to see a cure-all in organization now. If you become too methodical, make time for some leisure. Stop worrying about the schedule and remember that things cannot always be planned out; sometimes it is best to relax. A mind that is at ease can often see the future clearly and choose the shortest route to a goal.

Your objective: **Keep things rolling without over-organizing or getting into a rut. When working with others, find a common approach that is efficient but allows for occasional diversions so that they will not be tempted to take off on their own.**

You want to get things going — speed up a project — and feel that tedious conversations are a waste of time; you would rather jump headfirst into a job and get fast action. Those close to you probably appreciate your desire to press forward, but they will caution you not to be too impatient. They sense your tendency to be hasty now — and your suppressed need for rest.

Actually, your current zeal for progress is partly caused by a feeling that you must drive yourself. Deep down, you know that you are not as amibitious as you like to appear. You feel that you must move very fast if you are to overcome your natural slowness. However, if you keep trying for a few weeks, and avoid extreme hastiness, one day you will realize that there is no need to push for fast action because you are getting things done.

Your movements reflect the lackadaisical attitudes you are trying to correct. Make your body move more quickly.

While you are learning how to make progress, you may overestimate the value of speed. If you suspect that you have become too impatient or pushy, slow down. Put aside your ambitions occasionally and make sure that you are getting enough rest. Otherwise you may find that slowly plodding people get ahead faster than you do. They rested while you were straining — then overtook you when you were tired. The fastest way is often the steady, unhurried way.

Your objective: **Proceed swiftly but patiently. Be goal-orientated without becoming hasty. In your dealings with others, work out a mutual approach that is purposeful but not over-ambitious, so that there will be no need to push them.**

Your present wish is to be tough and independent — to claim your share of life without asking permission from anyone. Since you are so preoccupied with self-reliance now, you may be surprised that others do not share your interest. But most people are not trying to cope with secret feelings of weakness — as you are.

How can you create an atmosphere where firmness prevails? Softening influences may be in your environment, but they are also in yourself. Some of your old attitudes are still quite ineffectual. You dislike weakness because you cannot always control your own emotions or stand up for your rights. Keep trying, though, and in a few weeks, you will gain the necessary inner strength; then you will no longer need to display your toughness.

You must strengthen your body too. Change your lax movements into more purposeful, energetic ones.

In your search for a more determined attitude, you may become too grim or hard-hearted. To prevent this, make a point of being gentle, friendly and of enjoying harmless fun now and then. If you rediscover the joy in life, you will strengthen yourself for the times when determined effort is necessary. Adopt goals that are dictated by inner strength, not a power-hungry ego. Demand your fair share, of course.

Your objective: **Be strong without becoming inconsiderate towards the world and yourself. Others will go along with you if you use an approach that encourages strength in a reasonable and amiable way.**

You want to forge ahead now and reach your goal through determination rather than strategy. You think it below your dignity to compromise or evade problems. The people you love will probably encourage your efforts to stand up to challenges, but they will also warn you not to become too stubborn. They know that you tend to throw your weight around at the moment.

You like to be considered a determined person, but in the past you have really been quite indecisive. Your outward contempt for evasiveness or compromise stems in part from your inner fear that you are too easygoing — unable to deal with the obstacles ahead of you. Since you are unsure of your own strength, you feel that you must guard against any show of weakness. It will take you a few weeks to develop the determined attitude you desire, but with practice, you will; decisiveness will then come easily for you.

Your hesitant body movements betray a lack of strength and character. Try to move more energetically.

Until you learn how to forge ahead naturally, you may overshoot the goal sometimes and become too rough and tough. That is the time to bring some diplomacy into play. Let things flow of their own accord temporarily; do not force them. Try to strengthen your position through negotiation. In this way, you can gain impact for those times when an obstruction must be removed by force.

Your objective: **Learn to be flexible in the use of power. Proceed with determination but do not waste your energy. You will encounter a growing number of obstacles if you force your way. When dealing with others, keep your purpose in mind, but proceed with ease, so that they will not be forced into a devious, evasive role.**

Right now you feel that you are being prohibited from unfolding your personality and denied the things you deserve just because of certain traditions. You think that conventional law and order are sometimes too restrictive for the truly dynamic. Others may encourage your attempts to be forceful, but they also fear that your preoccupation with self-expression will lead you to reactions that border on the criminal.

Actually, your zeal to break up the existing order is caused, in part, by your unsuccessful attempts to overcome the restraints and inhibitions within yourself. You are blaming outside formalities for your own inner difficulties in expressing strong feelings. It will take several weeks of continued effort to overcome your old, constrained attitudes. But once you do, the need to act as an outlaw will disappear.

Your stiff habits are evident in your body coordination; try to move in a less controlled, more dynamic manner.

Until forceful behaviour becomes second nature to you, you may break some rules or overturn some traditions needlessly. You can avoid this by trying to evaluate things impartially. Look for the reasons behind the existing order; then proceed with energetic — but justified — action. You should have little trouble if you simply wish to grow and expand, but if you try to develop yourself at the expense of others, you will find serious obstructions.

Your objective: **Be dynamic but just. Break only those rules that are obviously unfair or obsolete. Others will support you if they feel that your dynamic projects will not hurt them.**

At present you want to face a danger head-on and make a wholehearted attempt to get what you want. You are willing to take great risks, and you are impatient with the compromise and caution practised by others. Your friends may encourage your brave ideals, but they can also see that your preoccupation with courage is a compensation for some hidden fear.

Although you are more daring now than you used to be, some of your habits are still quite timid; this inner lack of power is causing your present need for direct, forceful action. Before you can do away with the weakness and compromises around you, you must develop your own strength. It will take a few weeks, but one day — after you have conquered your old, fearful attitudes — the courage you desire will come naturally.

A lack of forcefulness is noticeable in your gestures lately; try to move more energetically.

Your attempts to become fearless may be exaggerated for a while. If you find yourself being heartless, bring some gentleness back into your life; do peaceful things occasionally, unrelated to the power-struggle. When you take your mind off a conflict, you are often better able to see real issues and resolve deadlocks. Perhaps you were once too cautious when forceful action was needed; now you are trying to hide your doubts behind a tough front. But the truly courageous person is also gentle.

Your objective: **Be fearless and dynamic without becoming inconsiderate. Your present struggle will be more successful if you use tact and intelligence. In your relations with others you can overcome their reluctance by finding an approach that faces the issues in a subtle way.**

At the moment you want to push a project through in spite of discouraging circumstances. You feel that, with enough effort, most battles can be won.

You may not be aware that some of your own discouraged and tired habits are major obstacles in your path. You dislike defeatism partly because you have not overcome your own pessimism. You are willing to take desperate measures because you think you cannot win otherwise. Yet these desperate, unthinking actions are self-defeating. It will be a few weeks before you gather enough faith in yourself to succeed. But keep trying, and one day you will realize that you have conquered your hidden resignation. Then you will no longer need to push ahead recklessly.

Your sluggish body movements betray your lack of conviction. Try to move with more vigour.

Until determined effort comes naturally, you may sometimes overshoot the mark and be too bold or demanding. When this happens, practise humility and patience for a change. Take time out to rest and do things for other people; make sure that your projects are basically sound and that you have enough support to carry them out. A desire for self-reliance is probably behind your actions now. This is a worthy goal, but do not succumb to the temptation to push weaker people aside. Only a bully feels that he must be ruthless to get what he wants.

Your objective: **Stick to your goal without becoming a demanding egotist. Do not exhaust your energies and the patience of others through an over-aggressive attitude. Others will co-operate with you if they see that you get results without hurting them.**

Right now you want to be free of all weaknesses — forceful, strong in mind and body and prepared for the struggle ahead. You recognize others' soft spots easily and think that they too want to toughen up. However, most people will show little interest in the subject since they have no need to overcome a secret feeling of helplessness — as you do. Your friends will encourage you to be more firm, but they will also warn you not to be too impatient with yourself or others; they sense that your hidden softness can anger and frustrate you now.

Before you can get the things outside you under control, you must control yourself; some of your attitudes are still rather lax and irresolute. It will take a few weeks to conquer the softness within, but when you do, you will eliminate your fear of chaos outside.

Your physical movements betray your lack of energy and purpose. Cultivate these qualities as you walk, sit or stand and you will feel better.

While you are learning to overcome your weaknesses, you may become too hard on yourself and the world. Correct this by taking time out to do some harmless, relaxing things; let yourself show tender feelings once in a while. Such moments will refresh and strengthen you. Remember that a weakness is not necessarily a disgrace, but if you act strong when you are not, you may find yourself in humiliating positions.

Your objective: **Develop a dynamic attitude but remember your weaknesses. You can get things done without becoming angry, tense or exhausted. When working with others, allow for a relaxed approach that makes them enjoy the effort.**

You would like to engage in some unprecedented, daring activity now. You feel that life is too short to be wasted on monotonous work and that few things can be won by patience. Your loved ones will probably encourage your attempts to start new projects, but they will also urge you to take things more slowly. They can see that you are driving yourself too hard — trying to make up for your hidden lack of energy.

In spite of the outside circumstances that seem to dampen your initiative, your own lack of pep is the main reason that your environment seems so dull at the moment. Before you can lead an exciting life, you must rouse yourself. It will take you a few weeks to overcome your passive, tired habits, but one day you will realize that you have learned how to get things moving; then you will no longer need to push yourself — and others — so hard.

Your languid body movements are at odds with your need to be more aggressive. Try to move quickly and lightly.

Until an enterprising attitude comes naturally to you, you will go overboard at times and become angry or demanding. When this happens, practise the qualities you have neglected — such as patience and consistency. Do some steady, relaxing work; stop trying to turn the world upside down. You do not have to show initiative all the time; energy must be allowed to renew itself.

Your objective: **Get your projects under way and nurse them along patiently, so that you have enough energy left to finish them. Do not expect too much too soon and avoid accidents. The people you depend on will show more initiative when they see that your approach is gradual.**

<table><tr><td>**41**</td><td>*REASON*</td><td></td><td></td></tr></table>

You want to form all your opinions on the basis of facts now. You think that reason holds the key to understanding while imagination leads to pleasant, but mistaken, beliefs. Those close to you will probably approve of your efforts to be correct and factual, but they will also warn you that you cannot shut out all emotions.

You like to be considered a sober person, and to some extent you are. However, many of your old attitudes are still quite irrational. Your feelings sometimes obscure your reason, and you cannot always distinguish between fact and fiction. Your unruly emotions are the main reason that you find it difficult to deal with unruly people or forces outside you. But if you keep trying, in a few weeks you will learn when and where to show emotion — and when to be objective.

Your body movements betray a lack of discipline. Try to move in a more controlled way.

Your present need for a reasoning attitude may carry you away in the coming weeks, and you may find yourself becoming too strict and cold. You can easily change this by bringing some kindness and originality back into your life. Let yourself show affection and sentiment sometimes. Allow your heart to express itself so that you can think more clearly later, undisturbed by repressed emotions. A person who never expresses his feelings is not reasonable; he is merely cold and stuffy.

Your objective: **Use your reason in a natural way, without stifling your emotions or spoiling all the fun. Let the 'child within you' express itself now and then. Others will play along with you if you approach mutual projects with cheerful imagination.**

At the moment you would like things to stay just as they are; you seek eternal truths rather than transitory benefits, and you think that people who often change their ways are superficial or dishonest. The people you love will undoubtedly encourage your attempts to stabilize things, but they are also worried that you will get left behind as the world moves on.

Actually, your interest in stability stems from your need to find a firm foothold in life for yourself. Some of your old habits are still rather fickle and unsteady. Your dislike for progress stems, in part, from your own inclinations toward opportunism. Your inner struggle between a need for stability and a desire to push ahead is causing you more difficulty than any outside forces. It will take you a few weeks to gain the settled position you are seeking, but once you do, your uneasiness over changes and flux will disappear.

One part of yourself that is obviously restless is your body; try to stand more erectly and move more firmly.

Until you feel more secure, you may exaggerate the quality and become stagnant or inhibited. If this happens, make it a point to look ahead sometimes and to make necessary changes. By taking care of the future, you will set the stage for a truly stable life. You feel threatened by change now, but you must move with the times to some extent.

Your objective: **Proceed steadily and make needed changes without disregarding the need for stability. See the future as an opportunity to stabilize conditions. Arrange matters so that others can maintain basic principles and resist superficial influences while at the same time keeping up with the times.**

Your strongest wish right now is to maintain an impartial, just attitude. You believe that there is no sense in getting angry or impatient when differences can be settled fairly, according to established rules. Your attempts to be just are probably appreciated by those around you, but at the same time they will let you know that you are not being forceful enough. They sense your tendency to become inhibited – and your hidden hostility.

Although you are often shocked by the violence and injustice around you, there is a good deal of violence in yourself. Deep down, you want to break the rules too. You feel that you must keep yourself — and the world — on very tight reins or anarchy and chaos will break out. It will take you a few weeks to conquer these hostile instincts, but if you keep trying, you will be able to overcome them. Then justice will not seem so all-important.

Your fidgety body movements betray your hidden aggressiveness. Try to stand straighter and move more smoothly.

While you are learning to control your belligerence, you may swing to another extreme and become too restrained or timid. That is the time to allow yourself some legitimate self-expression. Do things that require forceful action; make sure that your rules are not stifling you. Instead of suppressing your hostility, direct the energy it gives you into civilized channels.

Your objective: **Be just and fair without becoming inhibited. Your attitude can be dynamic and considerate at the same time. When you have to deal with unreasonable people who keep breaking the rules, allow them to let off steam in an orderly and constructive way.**

At present you want to be upright and truthful; you are trying to avoid weakness or compromise and you feel that people of integrity must not be swayed by flattery, favours or a need for approval. You may be surprised that most other people do not share your deep concern for firmness; that is because they do not feel as weak as you secretly do.

In many respects, you are the strong person that you would like to be, but some of your attitudes are not as firm as you think. It is often difficult for you to pick out the truth and to acknowledge it honestly. Since you feel so weak, you are trying to surround yourself with rigid principles that will keep you — and those around you — on the straight and narrow. It will take you a few weeks to build the inner strength you need. When you do, you will feel strong enough to be flexible.

Your limp body movements indicate your present lack of character. Straighten your backbone — literally.

Until firmness becomes second nature to you, you may go overboard and become stiff and dogmatic at times. Avoid this by practising tact and tolerance occasionally. Stop measuring everyone by your own yardstick. Make your own rules for conduct clear, of course, but consider other people's needs too. Honest principles are needed as guidelines, but if your rules are too rigid; you will have to discard them often — and despise yourself for doing so.

Your objective: **Know what you want but take different points of view into consideration. Make your position clear but avoid calling everything 'by its right name'. Others will show more backbone if you conduct mutual projects in a firm but considerate manner.**

At the moment you want to endure difficulties with pride and self-confidence. You would like to stand on your own two feet and you feel that independence has to be earned through courage and strength of character. The people you love will probably approve of your attempts to be more confident, but they also sense that you are trying to camouflage a hidden uncertainty now.

You may feel that you have been placed in humiliating circumstances lately. However, the seeds of your lack of confidence are in yourself. Deep inside, you are feeling depressed and defeated. Your own inability to stand up to challenges is the main reason behind your present concern with confidence. It will take you a few weeks to regain your faith in yourself, but once you do, you will no longer fear discouragement and dependence.

Although your mind has grasped the idea of confidence, your body is still moving slowly and sluggishly; try to move with more vigour.

While you are trying to change your old, discouraged attitudes, you may become over-confident or arrogant. If this happens, practise some of the qualities you have been neglecting — such as modesty and patience. Admit your shortcomings, and try to work around them. If you discover the weak points in the structure of your life, you can strengthen them; then your self-confidence and hopes for independence will be well-founded.

Your objective: **Build your faith and independence on a solid foundation, be confident without becoming over-confident. If others seem discouraged and/or submissive, work out a mutual plan that is basically confident but acknowledges weak areas.**

You would like to present a strong-willed, decisive face to the world right now. You want to make up your mind about long-neglected matters and act without procrastination or evasion. Those you love will probably encourage your attempts to face important issues, but they also feel that you have lost your ability to relax. They know that you are trying too hard to overcome a hidden reluctance to make up your mind.

Although you are often annoyed by the vacillation around you, deep down you know that you, too, are plagued by indifference and indecision. Too often you postpone decisions rather than take action; then you worry about all the things still left to be done. Until you shed these delaying tactics, you will not feel able to make clear-headed decisions. If you keep trying, though, in a few weeks you will develop the necessary confidence in your judgment. Then your preoccupation with decisiveness will disappear.

Your sleepy body movements have probably bothered you lately. Make yourself move more alertly.

You may overshoot your goal sometimes and become stubborn or arrogant about your decisions. Regain your balance by taking time out to relax with friends occasionally. Do not try to be alert every moment — noticing and judging everything; let your thoughts and decisions flow naturally from the circumstances.

Your objective: **Decide issues one at a time, without arrogance or prejudice. Learn to maintain an attitude of restful alertness. If others seem indifferent, find a common approach which provides for easy decision-making on all levels and stimulates their pride.**

You are trying to clarify obscure ideas and situations now so that accuracy, honesty and order can be re-established in your life. Wherever you find confusion — in your environment, among your possessions, in other people, etc. — you will try to correct it.

What you are probably less willing to admit is that disorder also exists within yourself. Some of your old attitudes are rather confused and undisciplined; part of your fear of clutter and disarray stems from your frustration at your inability to arrange your own affairs. Before you can organize the things around you, you will have to clear up the confusion inside yourself. This will take you a few weeks, but with continued effort, you will be able to sort out your feelings. A disorderly environment will not bother you so much then — you will know that you can handle it.

You have probably noticed that your body tends to slump or move spasmodically. Try to make your movements smoother — more in tune with your wish for order.

While you are trying to establish a well-regulated system, you may fall into the extremes of rigidity or stiffness. If this happens, bring some flexibility back into your life. Enjoy relaxed, informal surroundings; drop some of your prejudices and open your mind to alternative solutions. Shake up your present system so that you can arrive at a final order that is in harmony with your nature.

Your objective: **Help things find their own form, let a structure develop from within. You can be orderly without becoming narrow-minded and suspicious. When working with others, organize your projects in a way that allows them to follow a general pattern without needless supervision.**

Your present desire is to act cautiously — to base your opinions on experience rather than impulse. You think that many of the people around you are gullible and childish, and you are surprised that they do not try to develop a more reserved attitude. However, most people think you are being too critical now; they sense that you tend to disbelieve everything because you are afraid of your hidden emotions.

Your search for wisdom is not being frustrated by your environment, but by yourself. In spite of your efforts to be cool and detached, you still get involved with people and projects too easily. To protect yourself from being carried away by everything, you have decided not to trust anything. It will take you a few weeks to overcome the naïvety that is at the heart of your problem, but once you do, you will no longer need to be so sceptical.

Your uncontrolled body movements betray your hidden immaturity; move with more reserve and you will feel more reserved.

Until you develop the experienced attitude you are seeking, you may overdo things and become too cynical. If this happens, bring some spontaneity back into your life. Express your feelings openly sometimes; believe things that sound reasonable even if they cannot be proved. If you release your suppressed emotions, you will free yourself to develop a healthy scepticism.

Your objective: Show your feelings spontaneously without getting carried away by naïve impulses and childish hopes. Reserve the right to think, but also get involved and enjoy life. If others seem silly, adopt a mutual plan that is reasonable yet allows for spontaneity.

Right now you want to lead a reserved, dignified life, free of haste and senseless activity. If you cannot avoid being rushed, you try to develop a mental detachment, reminding yourself that you will be able to relax later. To those around you, your attitude seems weary and artificial. They feel that you are putting on aristocratic airs to compensate for your suppressed urge to get ahead.

The factors that prevent you from leading a more dignified life are not only in your environment; some are in yourself. Deep down, you know that you are still quite impatient and restless. Part of your dislike for haste stems from your inability to remove yourself from the frantic pace around you. It will take you a few weeks to resolve the conflict between your desire for a quiet, dignified life and your urge to push ahead. However, with continued effort, you will be able to bring the two concepts into harmony.

You still move in a rushed, frenzied fashion. If you change this trait, you will begin to feel more dignified.

Until reserve and a slower pace come naturally to you, you may become withdrawn or apathetic. If this happens, remember the need for ambitious activity once in a while. Take advantage of opportunities; provide for your economic security. With the future assured, you will be in a better position to enjoy the leisurely life and dignified activities that you are seeking.

Your objective: **Learn to get ahead without losing your dignity. Attend to the basic daily needs like a gentleman (or lady). When others seem pushy, work out a common approach that satisfies their ambition in a dignified way.**

Your goal at the moment is consideration. You do not want to hurt or offend anybody and you try to reward cruelty with kindness. Those close to you will encourage your benevolent efforts, but they will also warn you not to become too permissive. They sense that you are trying to cope with your hidden hostility by avoiding all conflicts.

Deep down, you know that you still want to exercise your power too forcefully; you are often demanding and inconsiderate. Your zeal for gentleness — in yourself and others — is partly caused by your inability to control these traits. But before you can expect gentleness in others, you will have to cultivate it in yourself. It will take you a few weeks to reach the mental state you are striving for. However, one day you will realize that you have overcome the ruthlessness within you; gentleness will then come naturally.

Your hidden attitude shows in your belligerent body movements. Try to make your movements softer, more yielding.

You may see a cure-all in benevolence now. If you find yourself becoming powerless, bring some courage back into your life. Daring, aggressive things must be done occasionally; do them, even if it startles people. Defend your legitimate rights against attack and develop a strong position for yourself. Then you can afford to treat the world, and yourself, with generosity and forgiveness.

Your objective: **Be gentle without becoming ineffectual or permissive. Your attitude can be considerate and courageous at the same time. When others seem hostile, work out a mutual plan that is subtle yet dynamic, so that they can drop their aggressive pose.**

You are trying to be tolerant and understanding now. You feel that truth can be looked at from several angles and you want to avoid rigid principles and fanatical beliefs. Your loved ones will appreciate your attempts to be more sympathetic, but they will also warn you against losing all character. They sense that your preoccupation with flexibility is an over-reaction to your own rigidity.

You find much narrow-mindedness and intolerance in your environment now, but these traits are also in yourself. Your hidden prejudices are the main obstacles in your path to a more liberal attitude; your uncompromising habits keep you from handling situations with understanding and tact. It will take you a few weeks to strike a balance between firmness and flexibility, but if you keep trying, you will be able to achieve it.

You can start by changing your stiff movements into more graceful, supple gestures.

In your efforts to become more open-minded, you may go overboard and become too pliable or vague in your beliefs. If this happens, try to be firm now and then. Set up some straightforward policies and make them clear to everyone. If you are secure about your basic principles, you will not be afraid to make exceptions occasionally. On the other hand, if order is not established, you — and others — will be tempted to stretch the truth.

Your objective: **Learn to be flexible without losing character. Establish firm guidelines but apply them with an open mind. In your dealings with others, find a common approach that is positive yet understanding, so that they can drop their rigid pose.**

At the moment you are trying to take life in your stride and bear calamities with a smile. You think that brooding is a kind of sickness and that most troubles come from taking life too seriously. You may be surprised that your friends and loved ones rarely join you in your laughter; they know that your jokes are a cover-up for your hidden sadness.

Although gloom seems to be coming at you from all sides, most of it is coming from yourself. You cannot seem to stop regretting, repenting and suffering, and you compensate for this by trying to find anything funny. It will be several weeks before you overcome the sadness inside you. But once you do, the need to poke fun at everything will disappear.

Although your mind understands the need for lightness, your body movements are still heavy and clumsy. Try to move more gracefully and you will feel less weighed down.

Until a more cheerful attitude is second nature to you, you may overestimate the value of humour and become cynical or frivolous. You must remember the need for serious concern. Take time out to contemplate your goals and the real meaning of life; show an interest in other people's troubles occasionally. If you acknowledge the existence of serious truths, sadness, and even tragedy, you can learn to deal with these things gracefully and with the best humour possible.

Your objective: **Take events in good humour without becoming indifferent to the outcome. Show concern for the more serious aspects without getting weighed down by them. After you have faced the underlying issues you will stop worrying anyway. If others seem worried, adopt a mutual plan that allows for humour but solves basic problems.**

You are trying to cultivate good form, fine manners and elegance now. You want everything to have a certain style and you are quick to notice any coarseness or vulgarity around you. Although the people you love will encourage your attempts to create a more refined atmosphere, they also feel that you are trying to impose an unnatural form on some things — and that you are not entirely sure of your own refinement.

While it is true that there is a lack of elegance in your environment, your dissatisfaction with yourself is the main reason for your preoccupation with refinement. You have not completely shed your own coarseness yet and, in many ways, you do not come up to your own high standards. You dislike boorish behaviour or flashy surroundings because they remind you of your imperfections. It will take you a few weeks to smooth out your rough spots, but one day you will realize that refined behaviour comes naturally to you.

Your body movements are still on the clumsy side. Try to move with more elegance and you will feel more elegant.

Your present interest in refinement may cause you to overshoot your goal and become affected. You can change this by bringing some informality back into your life. Relax with good friends sometimes; be yourself and enjoy spontaneous fun. Remember that the most beautiful forms complement nature.

Your objective: **Find a form that is natural. Refine things without ignoring or violating their nature. Culture and art gain meaning only if they complement the nature of things. If the people around you seem uncivilized or clumsy, find a common approach that is not opposed to their nature.**

You are trying to make life more interesting for yourself now. You want to be entertained, stimulated, and you try to avoid anything that is dull or tiresome. You find many of the people around you uninspiring, and you think that they would appreciate your thoughts on how to make themselves more interesting. However, your friends have no need to compensate for hidden boredom with a show of brilliance — as you do.

While it is true that a humdrum existence can take the spice out of life, your biggest problem is your own inability to entertain yourself. The diversions you plan are mere distractions; when they are over, you are left with your own dullness. It will take you some weeks to lift yourself out of your lethargy. However, keep pursuing your goal, and one day you will realize that you are interested in your life again — without artificial distractions.

One way to change your old mental habits is to change your languid physical habits. Move with more vigour and you will feel better.

While you are learning to find more inspiration around you, you may overdo things and become affected or caught up in superficial activity. That is the time to practice some of the qualities you have neglected, such as plain common sense. Enjoy simple, commonplace things occasionally. Take a good look at your life; you may find that it provides many interesting opportunities.

Your objective: **Find more inspiration in yourself, and enjoy the simple things of life. Dare to be simply 'you' and you will be interesting in the eyes of worthwhile people. If your present friends and colleagues seem plain and dull, discover a common goal that inspires all of you.**

Your current desire is to stress the serious, profound aspects of life; you think that true contentment comes only after suffering, and you suspect that most people have only the semblance of happiness. Your loved ones will probably encourage your attempts to look below the surface, but they also feel that you are being too solemn.

Actually, you are trying to compensate for your hidden frivolity at the moment. You know that you are susceptible to a careless, superficial way of life, and you are afraid that you will be carried away by it. Your concern with suffering is partly caused by your inability to feel real concern for others. It will take you a few weeks to overcome these shallow attitudes. However, one day you will realize that your thoughts and actions have gained depth without constant effort on your part.

Your vague, careless body movements betray your hidden lack of concern; try to put more weight and importance behind your gestures.

If you find that your interest in profound wisdom is making you too serious, try to bring some joy and optimism back into your life. Look at the light side of things occasionally and do not search for deep, dark reasons behind everything. If you let your mind come up for light and air, it will be able to recognize the truth more easily. If you don't, your soul-searching will turn into useless brooding.

Your objective: **What you need now is a happy medium that prevents optimism as well as soul-searching from going to excess. Learn to enjoy life without becoming frivolous or careless. If the foolish behaviour of some people bothers you, engage them in a worthwhile mutual project that they can enjoy.**

At the moment you would like to be satisfied with the status you have already achieved; you are seeking peace of soul, not material success; true happiness, you feel, comes from contemplation of the real meaning of life and a limitation of worldly desires. To your friends and loved ones, your ideas seem fatalistic and contrived. They sense that you are suppressing your urge to get ahead and that, as a result, you are bogged down in your 'profound' thoughts.

Try as you may, you cannot always keep your mind off superficial pursuits — greater status, a bigger house, etc. You dislike ambition in others because you, too, crave to be a success. Until you reconcile your need to get ahead with your desire for spiritual meditation, you will not be truly content. It will take a few weeks, but if you keep trying, you will be able to overcome the worst of your superficiality.

Your restless, erratic body movements give tangible evidence of your confusion. Try to move more calmly.

Until you have trained yourself to put ambition and contemplation in their proper places, you may overshoot your goal and become too resigned and too quick to give up a fight. Avoid this by bringing some optimism — and a little aggression — back into your life. Take time out from your thinking to satisfy your need for success. Remember that contemplation is not an end in itself.

Your objective: **Plan your moves thoroughly so that your success rests on a solid foundation. Your projects can be meaningful and ambitious at the same time. If others seem superficial to you, formulate a worthwhile common goal that engages their deeper feelings.**

Right now you think that you should not demand too much from life – that you should leave others a fair share. You try to forgive your opponents and to regard setbacks as blessings in disguise. You are surprised that others are so demanding. Your loved ones will warn you that you are becoming too permissive. They can see that you are trying to compensate for your hidden hostility by allowing yourself to be stepped on.

Actually, you are practising a false modesty. Deep down, some of your old attitudes are quite aggressive. You really feel little concern for the rights of others; you dislike inconsiderate behaviour because you cannot always check your own selfish instincts. Before you try to make the people around you more obliging, you will have to control your own arrogance. It will take you a few weeks to do this, but if you keep trying, you can overcome your hostile tendencies; then modesty will not seem so all-important.

Your body movements are still hard and impatient; try to move in a more relaxed, soft way.

While you are learning to become more unassuming, you may swing to another extreme and become too timid and submissive. If that happens, start to practise some determination for a change. Do things that require bold, daring action; demand your fair share. If you put yourself in a strong position, you will be better able to help the weak.

Your objective: **Forget meaningless arguments but defend your legitimate rights. The quiet life you desire will be yours after you face the challenges. You can be modest without becoming submissive. If people around you seem aggressive and egotistical, find a common goal that allows them to use their energies in more constructive ways.**

One of the qualities that you especially want to develop in yourself and others is humility. You think that true happiness comes from the suppression of ego and service to others. Although you appreciate receiving advice, you rarely give any for fear that it might be taken as criticism. You will find that few of the people around you are interested in becoming more humble; they do not have an excessive inner pride to overcome — as you do.

Your choice of symbols shows that your preoccupation with humility stems from your inability to control your own need to assert yourself; some of your attitudes are still quite haughty and vain. Before you can deal with the arrogance around you, you will have to become more humble yourself. It will take you a few weeks to learn to be more selfless, but as you do, your emphasis on humility will slowly recede into the background.

Your movements, too, are still rigid and assertive. Try to sit back and relax your body.

When you overdo your self-abasement, you may find that others take advantage of you. If this happens, do some things that require self-confidence and courage. Re-establish your self-respect, and others will respect you. Remember that the concepts of humility and self-confidence need not be opposites. In fact, the truly self-confident are invariably humble, and vice-versa.

Your objective: **Lose your ego without losing your self-respect. You can be humble without becoming servile. Try to understand others but do not sacrifice your deep convictions. If people around you seem domineering, find a mutual aim that allows them to express their self-confidence in a considerate way.**

You are trying to become more serious now; you want to devote yourself to worthy causes and important goals. You think that most people shun involvement with their fellow men, and you want to do your bit to reverse this trend. The people you love will encourage your efforts to be more concerned; however, they will also warn you not to feel too sorry for others — or for yourself. They sense your tendency to play the tragic hero.

Actually, your display of serious concern is a bit hypocritical at the moment. Deep down, you know that your greatest concern is with yourself; your preoccupation with devotion is partly caused by your inability to care strongly for anyone else. As long as you must make yourself feel pity, your understanding of others is artificial. But keep trying for a few weeks, and one day you will realize that your interest in the problems around you is serious. Then you will no longer seek causes to which you can devote yourself; they will come naturally to you.

Your light, careless body movements betray your shallow attitudes. Try to move with more weight and importance.

You may go overboard for a while and find yourself brooding about the world's ills. If this happens, try to redevelop your sense of humour. Take life philosophically sometimes. Learn to distinguish between the things that should be taken seriously and those which should be laughed off.

Your objective: **Devote yourself to a worthy cause but do not drown in heavy feelings. You can show concern without losing your sense of balance. If other people seem indifferent, develop a common approach that engages their critical intellect in a meaningful way.**

You have a strong desire to retreat from noise and confusion at the moment. You feel that the time has come for earnest self-examination and you do not want to dissipate your energy with frivolous diversions. Those close to you are worried over your tendency to take things too seriously now. They can tell that your need to be left alone with your thoughts is a symptom of your hidden confusion.

Although you are often disturbed by the chaos around you, the worst chaos is within yourself. You really find it difficult to concentrate on the serious matters you want to consider; your thoughts skip from subject to subject, and you are not sure of what is important and what is not. It will be a few weeks before these confused habits are completely controlled. However, one day you will realize that your thoughts are in order and concentration is easy for you. Outside noise and confusion will then stop frightening you.

Your body movements are still restless and erratic. Try to move more slowly and deliberately.

You may find yourself depressed or weighed down by a heavy conscience in the weeks ahead. Whenever this happens, bring some action and liveliness back into your life. Relax with your friends; laugh and have fun. Let your mind clear itself of heavy thoughts once in a while, and you will be better able to concentrate when you need to.

Your objective: **Your life can be full and exciting, and meaningful at the same time. Your thoughts can be lively and yet profound. If others seem irresponsible, add a touch of excitement to your common project, so that they can relate to it meaningfully.**

You are trying to look past superficial appearances and solve the hidden problems around you now. You want to cultivate compassion for the sick or helpless and you sometimes wonder how people can lead shallow, carefree lives when there is so much suffering in the world. Close friends will encourage your concern for others, but they also see your tendency to be too sentimental as a compensation for your lack of real concern.

You like to think of yourself as a sympathetic, deep-thinking person, and in many ways you are -- or at least you are trying to be. However, some of your attitudes are still superficial and indifferent. Part of your zeal to create a compassionate environment is caused by your own inability to see under the surface and truly be of help to others. It will take you a few weeks to learn how to care about -- and reach -- real problems, but with continued effort, you will eventually be able to.

Your body movements are still vague and careless; try to move in a more deliberate way.

While you are developing your ability to think and feel deeply, you may sometimes find yourself depressed. Avoid this by keeping some humour and nonchalance in your life. Do carefree and casual things occasionally; do not worry about anyone who does not worry about you. Try not to be presumptuous about digging into other people's problems; they will resent it.

Your objective: **Be concerned about the things that count but do not get weighed down. Go below the surface now and then but do not stay there. Others will get more involved in your mutual project if you drop your serious attitude and show a sense of proportion.**

At the moment you want to abandon all pretensions and lead a simple, down-to-earth life. You do not care to be burdened with soul-lifting aspirations; you just want to be yourself. Most of your friends find your ideas base and uninspiring. Your loved ones, especially, would appreciate a little more idealism on your part; they know that you look down on other people's pretentiousness and that you may sink too low in your efforts not to imitate them.

Although you want to appear natural, you have not quite succeeded yet. One reason that you are so disdainful of pretensions is that you are not immune to them yourself. Because you fear your tendency to become affected, you are trying to rid yourself of any trace of affectation — including all refined thoughts and actions. It will be a few weeks before you feel natural enough to allow yourself to be natural, but with continued effort, you can overcome your pretentiousness.

Your body still moves in the old, affected way. Let yourself move more naturally and you will feel more natural.

You may find that you have become too debased in the coming weeks; you can correct this by bringing some enthusiasm and idealism back into your life. Let yourself admire something beautiful, noble or inspired occasionally. A person who never shows admiration or enthusiasm is not natural; he is merely practising another affectation.

Your objective: **Be down-to-earth without neglecting the more sublime values and experiences that satisfy your higher needs. Drop your pretensions but remember your ideals. If others seem too idealistic or saintly, formulate a mutual aim that allows them to be natural on a higher level.**

<table><tr><td>72</td><td>DIVERSION</td><td>✓</td><td>—</td></tr></table>

Your present wish is to remove yourself from all competition. You want to relax, browse around and develop a versatile, imaginative approach to life. You are not interested in efficiency and speed; you feel that true happiness lies in the absence of strain. The people you love will encourage your efforts to stay out of a rut, but they will also urge you to adopt some concrete goals. They sense your lack of direction now.

You are bothered by the race for economic gain that is all around you. However, you know that you, too, are eaten up by worries about your future. One reason that you are trying so hard to protect yourself from pressure is that you are afraid that you will be drawn back into the rat race. It will be a few weeks before you shed your anxious habits. But once you do, your need for diversion will disappear.

If you make your hasty movements slower and more graceful, you will feel more relaxed.

Your search for diversion could lead you into irresponsibility. You can avoid this by incorporating some purpose and direction into your actions. Do some of the things you have felt too confused to do; take time out to plan for the future. Remember that the necessities of life must be provided for. If you try to ignore this truth, it will not go away but will simply nag at you from deep in your unconscious.

Your objective: Get out of the rut but do not forget your goal. Take care of the necessities in an open-minded way. Your worries will stop as soon as you have started to follow a clear plan. If the people you deal with seem one-track-minded, find a mutually satisfying approach that is goal-orientated in a relaxed way.

You have a strong desire to release tension and refrain from strenuous effort now. You want to forget past frictions, enjoy life, and you resent any attempts to dominate you or apply force in general. Your close friends will approve of your efforts to take things easy, but they will also warn you against a tendency to become too permissive.

Although there is some strain in your environment, the greatest tension is coming from within yourself. Deep down, some of your attitudes are quite domineering. You still want to fight for your rights — and win. Until you make peace between your superficial urge to relax and your hidden urge to fight, you cannot expect peaceful conditions around you. It will take you a few weeks to dissolve your inner tension, but as you do, your preoccupation with relaxation will gradually fade.

One part of yourself that especially needs to relax is your body. Right now your movements are very hard and aggressive.

If you find that you are overshooting your goal and becoming too soft and submissive, develop some strength of character as a balance. Do difficult things; satisfy your hidden urge to conquer occasionally. Clear up any conflicts around you quickly and wholeheartedly so that complete and immediate relief can occur. Small, nagging tensions can frustrate you more than the original problem.

Your objective: **Take it easy without becoming ineffective or helpless. Relax but be ready for unforeseen emergencies. Learn to be active without getting tense. In your dealings with others, work out a common approach that is easy-going but dynamic, so that nobody needs to push or get pushed.**

Right now you are trying to loosen up the stiffness around and inside you. You distrust established conventions; you want to be open-minded and understand things for yourself. However, you think that intellect alone is not always to be trusted — that sometimes we must act on instinct. Your loved ones may appreciate your attempts to become more adaptable, but they are often puzzled by your confused reasoning. They fear that you are overplaying the rôle of a nonconformist to compensate for your hidden rigidity.

You like to consider yourself a relaxed person, but in many ways you are still a prisoner of your own inhibitions. Deep down, you know that you still cannot judge ideas or individuals on their merits; you continue to be influenced by your preconceived notions. It will be several weeks before you can completely rid yourself of these prejudices, but when you do, you can begin to replace your rigid principles with a more realistic order.

Your stiff body movements indicate your hidden inhibitions. Try to move more loosely.

You may find that your efforts to understand and adapt to a new order cause your thoughts to become muddled and chaotic. If this happens, try to be more accurate and honest with yourself. Think things through instead of developing 'feelings' about them. Remember that the absence of all order is not freedom; it is merely anarchy.

Your objective: **Find the order that suits your nature and the nature of things. Instead of eliminating all inhibitions, simply lead a more open-minded life. When working with others, find a joint approach that is open-minded but structured, so that they can drop their preconceived ideas.**

Your present desire is to get away from your over-sophisticated, artificial surroundings and enjoy an unaffected way of life. You may even have some doubts about the usefulness of formal learning since it preserves the errors of the past as well as its wisdom. Your friends and loved ones may encourage your efforts to be less formal, but they will also warn you that you must practise some civilized customs in a civilized world. They sense your tendency to revert to barbarism as a camouflage for your own hidden affectations.

Although an unnatural environment irritates you, some of your own attitudes are quite artificial. Part of your zeal for spontaneity comes from your own inability to act naturally. As long as you must strive for informality, your actions will not be natural. Keep practising, though, and in a few weeks you will realize that you have found the way of life that best suits you; naturalness will then cease to be your dominating goal.

Your body movements are still affected; if you move more naturally you will feel more comfortable.

While you are trying to shed your affectations, you may become too coarse. If this happens, bring a little grace and elegance back into your life. Cultivate good form; satisfy your suppressed craving for refinement and you will be better able to enjoy a life that is natural, but not chaotic.

Your objective: **Gain freedom from superficial formalities by developing your own style. Get 'back to nature' in a sensible way, without neglecting the finer side of your personality. If some of the people around you seem reserved and stuffy, develop a common approach that is relaxed but respects their need for some formality.**

<table><tr><td>76</td><td>LIVELINESS</td><td>✓</td><td>✓</td></tr></table>

You would like to shake off gloomy thoughts and enjoy yourself now. Serious subjects depress you; you think you can come closer to truth and understanding by having a gay whirl and many friends. You may be surprised to find that few people share your taste for hectic activity. Only those who feel as weighed down as you do will be intrigued by your ideas; others sense your tendency to go to excesses now in an attempt to forget your hidden depression.

The gloom that disturbs you is not only outside yourself, but inside too. Deep down, you feel heavy and sluggish; you are bothered by unsettled problems and unable to shake off your lethargy and solve them. As long as these difficulties prey on your mind, you will not be completely happy. But if you keep trying to rouse yourself, one day you will find that your deep depression has disappeared. Then you will be able to think more clearly.

Your heavy, dragging body movements betray the burden your mind is carrying. Try to move more lightly, and your mind will feel lighter.

You may exaggerate your good intentions and find yourself engaging in chaotic, confused activities. If this happens, bring some seriousness back into your life. Search for the deeper meaning of life occasionally; remember your responsibilities. Face the truth, eventually, even if it is depressing, and try to build a solid foundation for your happiness.

Your objective: **Be lively without neglecting the deeper aspects. By first settling serious questions in your mind you can get ready for a carefree and exciting life. If others seem too concerned, approach your mutual projects in a relaxed but thorough manner.**

You feel stifled by monotonous tasks that are constant but uninspiring; you would like to stir things up, put new and daring ideas into practice. The people you love will probably encourage your attempts to make your life more exciting, but they are also worried that you will go overboard and create total chaos.

Although your routine may be dull, a large factor in your need for stimulation is your secret belief that you are dull and uninspired. You would like to go a little wild, but old habits and attitudes prevent you from taking action. Deep inside, you feel that this is the wrong time to make major changes. Thus your outer craving for excitement is fighting with your inner reluctance to disturb the established routine — and nothing gets done. It will take you a few weeks to resolve this conflict, but once you do, your life will not seem so stagnant.

Your physical lethargy is probably bothering you too; try to move with more life and energy.

You may find that your attempts to vary your routine make you and your surroundings disorganized and disturbed. If this happens, practise moderation now and then. Enjoy some things as they are; do not try to change everything. By settling down once in a while, you will be better able to see which things should be shaken up, and which left alone. Plan large changes in advance and effect them gradually.

Your objective: **Stir things up and make your life exciting, but do not go too far. You can join the fun and yet keep your inner balance. When dealing with others, explain needed changes to all involved, so that nobody gets shocked or confused.**

<table><tr><td>81</td><td>CALMNESS</td><td>⌣</td><td>⌢</td></tr></table>

Your present desire is to stay calm and undisturbed. You feel that there are few things worth getting excited about and that people who get carried away with enthusiasm are emotional and childish. Those close to you will appreciate your efforts to stay cool and detached, but they also fear that you are losing interest in them and the world around you.

Actually, some of your old habits are still quite undisciplined. You dislike emotional behaviour in others partly because you cannot always conceal your own feelings. Since you fear your emotional nature, you think you must suppress it entirely. It will be a few weeks before you can strike the necessary balance between spontaneity and calm, but the objectivity you are developing now is a step in the right direction. Once you have your feelings under control, your fear of emotional outbursts will disappear.

Your body movements still tend to be jumpy and disjointed. Try to move more gracefully — more in tune with your serene ideal.

Until calmness becomes habitual with you, you may over-shoot your goal and become too dull — bored and boring. You can correct this by putting some curiosity and interest back into practice. Take time to show concern for the world and those around you and do not try to stifle all of your feelings all of the time. If you do, these suppressed emotions will continue to disturb your peace of mind.

Your objective: **Balance your life without making it dull and without stifling the child within you. Be curious about things, but do not get carried away by naïve exuberance. When working with others, encourage them to express their feelings, but calmly, like adults.**

At the moment you want to slow down, drop out of the hustle and bustle that prevails around you. You think that opportunities are not going to run away, and that many people are pursuing goals in which they are not really interested. You will find that few of your friends arc interested in your ideas on the necessity of rest and relaxation; most people have not lost their sense of direction and purpose —as you have.

The pace around you may be frantic, but it is your own inability to slow down that bothers you most now. At rare moments you do take things easy, but most of the time you are rushing around impatiently. You cannot decide whether you want to rest or press forward, so you can enjoy neither work nor play. It will take a few weeks to resolve this conflict, but when you do you will find that a great deal of leisure is not so important to you; you can relax without it.

Even your body movements are hasty and nervous. Try to move more calmly and patiently.

While you are learning how to slow down, you may go to another extreme and become lazy or neglectful of your duties. If this happens, remember the need for ambition occasionally. Find the forgotten purpose in your life; fix a goal and concentrate on attaining it. By following a definite plan, you will be able to enjoy your leisure with a clear conscience.

Your objective: **Move ahead steadily, without excessive ambition or prolonged inactivity. You can be active in a leisurely way, and avoid haste and needless worry. When working with others, work out a common plan that has purpose and direction yet, at the same time, avoids hectic activity and allows periods of leisure.**

Right now you want to let things take their own course. You feel that people and projects must not be hurried and you avoid getting angry or impatient under any circumstances. Most people find your attitudes too passive; they feel that you should be more enterprising. However, those closest to you realize that your patient behaviour is really a pose — a compensation for your hidden urge to force things through.

Although your intentions are commendable, some of your old attitudes are really quite demanding. Deep down, you want to get tough — demand results — but you feel that such actions are inappropriate. The conflict between your urge to get angry and your feeling that you should practise quiet endurance is causing much of your present dissatisfaction. However, if you try to stay calm for the next few weeks, one day you will realize that your anger is under control.

Your body movements are still tense and hard. By changing this physical habit, you will take the first step toward becoming more patient.

You may overdo your efforts and become too permissive — too ready to give up without a fight. To avoid this, bring some initiative back into your life; push a project through occasionally; satisfy the adventurer in yourself. If you fulfil your suppressed ambitions occasionally, you will find it easier to be patient.

Your objective: **Have the initiative to start projects and the patience to carry them through. Know how to relax but do not become the passive object of circumstances. In your dealings with others, allow for gradual progress after the initial push, and let them participate constructively.**

Peace of mind is the quality you most value at present. Consequently, you are trying to avoid situations that require ambition, excellence or decisive leadership: You just want to live a quiet, unassuming life. The people you love will understand your need for rest; they can sense the tension inside you. However, they will also warn you against becoming too indifferent to the world around you.

Your search for peace of mind is really an attempt to withdraw from disappointing conditions. Some of your great expectations did not come true, and you are now trying to abandon them – and all ambition. But somewhere in the back of your mind you are holding on to these old, exaggerated hopes. You will not rest until you resolve this inner conflict by setting new, more realistic goals for yourself. When you do, you will realize that you no longer seek peaceful surroundings because you are at peace with yourself.

One part of you that is obviously still tense is your body; try to move in a calmer, more relaxed way.

You may find yourself exaggerating your need for a quiet, unstrained life in the weeks ahead. If you feel that you have become too indecisive or withdrawn, make it a point to be alert and firm occasionally. Decide the relative merits of things; face the issues of the day. Remember that new opportunities will appear, and keep an eye out for them.

Your objective: **Make decisions easily as they come up, so that no needless tensions develop. Practise 'restful alertness'. When involved with others, let the mutual project develop gradually, but provide for needed decisions and leadership.**

<table><tr><td>85</td><td>PLAINNESS</td><td>⚊</td><td>☷</td></tr></table>

You want to take a simple, common-sense approach to life at the moment. You feel that there is no need for displays of sophistication or intellectual ability — that people only engage in these things to impress others. You may also feel worn out and in need of rest. The people you love will probably encourage your unpretentiousness, but they will also let you know that they find you rather boring right now. They feel that you have lost interest in the little mental and physical niceties that make life interesting.

Although you are often irritated by the unnecessary frills and luxuries around you, your biggest problem is your own inability to act naturally and live simply. You are still tempted to dazzle others with your intellectual brilliance and impress them with your sophistication. It will take you a few weeks to overcome the hidden affectations, but when you do, common sense and simplicity will cease to be your dominating goals.

Your body movements are still quite affected. Try to move more naturally.

You may overestimate the value of a plain life and become dull and uninteresting for a while. If this happens, make it a point to liven up your routine. Let your imagination play with some thoughts; entertain and be entertained. By keeping your interest and intellect alive, you can make a good impression on others without play-acting.

Your objective: **Drop your affected habits, but develop your real interests. Provide for occasional inspiration while maintaining your inner balance. In your work with others you can avoid boring them by developing a common approach that is stimulating as well as down-to-earth.**

You are trying to avoid being troubled or emotionally involved with the suffering of others now. You think that too many people get carried away by petty sentimentality and take on burdens that do not belong to them. You may be surprised that few of your friends are interested in your ideas on how to stay peaceful and unworried. Those you love, especially, would appreciate a little more sympathy from you.

Actually, not all of the depressing influences that bother you are in your environment. Beneath your nonchalance, you feel very sad. You cannot stop brooding over the problems around you, and you are afraid that they are going to sink you. You feel that you can only stay afloat by sheer will-power — and by refusing to think of anything that reminds you of misfortune. It will take you a few weeks to learn how to handle these problems, but when you do, you will no longer fear trouble — your own or others'.

Your body still looks heavy and burdened. Try to move more lightly and you will feel less weighed down.

While you are learning how to direct your concern, you may sometimes become careless or superficial. That is the time to bring some depth and sympathy back into your life. Think about important issues; let yourself have deep feelings. Once you acknowledge the more profound — even tragic — aspects of life, you can start to overcome your fear of them.

Your objective: **Maintain peace of mind without becoming shallow. Show concern but do not get involved in petty sentiments or imaginary problems. If others seem over-concerned, find a common approach that faces basic truths but offers peace of mind and inner balance.**

You want to live a calm, subdued life now, free of excesses or undue excitement. You think that many people engage in a frantic pursuit of happiness, unaware that true joy thrives in a quiet atmosphere. Others find you a little tiresome at the moment; they sense your tendency to be indifferent to many things – and your hidden confusion.

Though the confusion in your environment disturbs you, there are problems in yourself too. Deep down, you have an urge to do wild, extravagant things. You know that you are not immune to excesses, so you are afraid to depart from the strict limits you have set for yourself. Your buried, immoderate impulses are fighting with your surface desires for peace and quiet. The emotional storm this creates is much more intense than any outside disturbance. It will take you several weeks to bring these contradictory desires into harmony, but when you do, moderation will no longer seem so important.

Your body movements are still disjointed, betraying your hidden confusion. Try to move in a calm, quiet way.

You may overshoot your goal in the coming weeks and find yourself bored and dull. If this happens, break the monotony occasionally; let your imagination play; do some exciting things. Find acceptable ways to express your hidden drives, and you will be better able to enjoy quiet happiness.

Your objective: **Develop a sensible interest in life that leads neither to excess nor to boredom. Practise moderation without becoming dull. When dealing with others, find a common approach that is reasonable but at the same time exciting.**